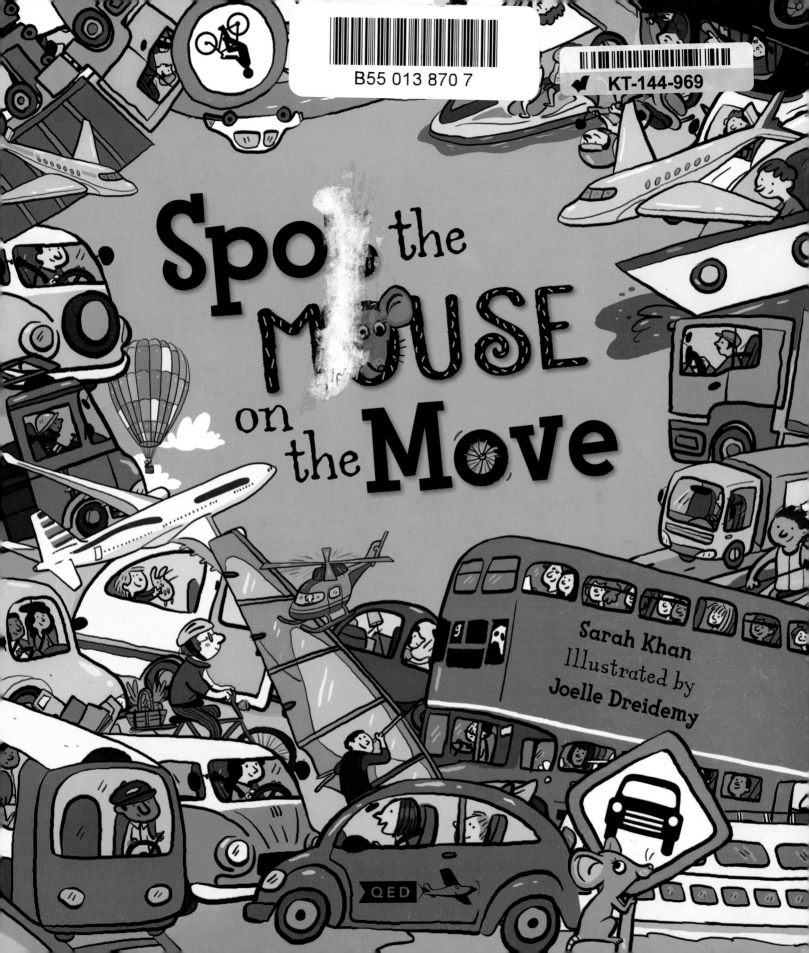

Spot the MOUSE on the Move

Sarah Khan

Illustrated by
Joelle Dreidemy

Airport

Harbour

Ferry

Spaghetti junction

Trains

This little mouse is hiding inside the book. Can you find him in every scene?

The MS Ulysses is one of
the world's largest ferries.
It has 12 decks and can
carry 1500 vehicles.

The world's smallest caravan is slightly larger than a single bed and can be towed at a top speed of 6mph.

Can you spot these things?

bench   balloon   burger   newspaper   guitar

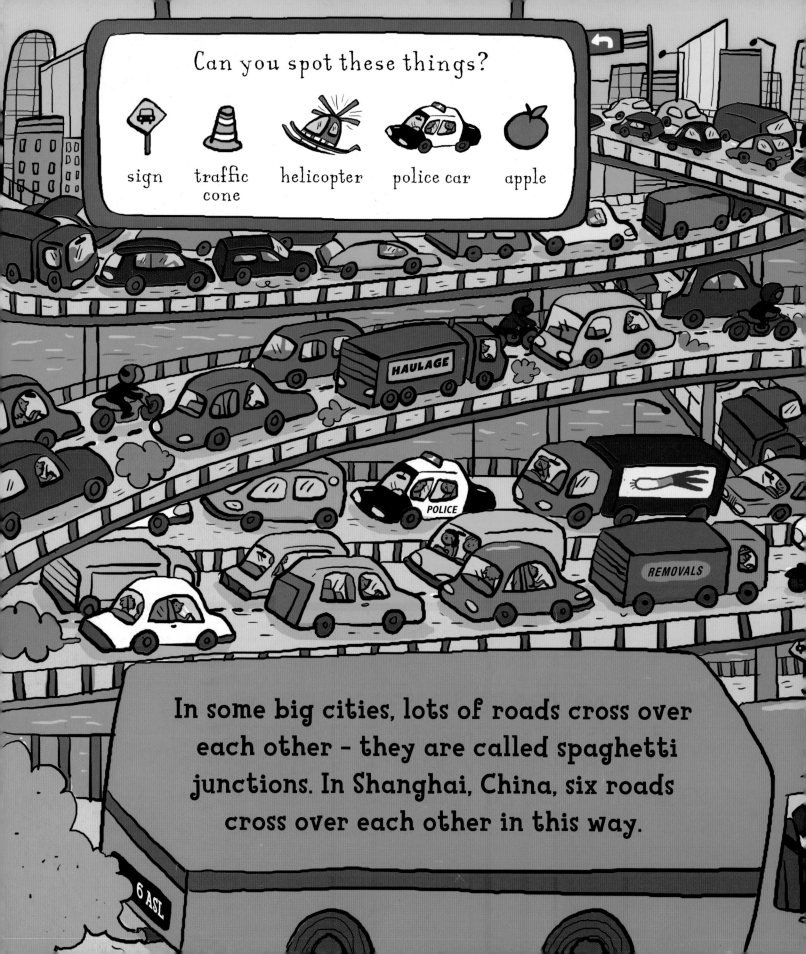

Can you spot these things?

sign · traffic cone · helicopter · police car · apple

In some big cities, lots of roads cross over each other - they are called spaghetti junctions. In Shanghai, China, six roads cross over each other in this way.

Trains used to be powered by steam but, these days, most run on diesel or electricity.

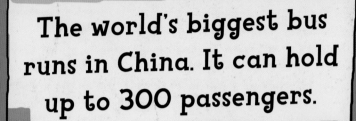

The world's biggest bus runs in China. It can hold up to 300 passengers.

What is your favourite way to travel?

Can you spot these things?

guinea pig   crayon   bow   pink headphones   sandwich

Can you spot these things?

message in a bottle

wheel

fishing net

blue crab

worms

One of the world's largest harbours is in San Francisco, USA. All kinds of boats sail in and out of the harbour, from tiny fishing boats to massive container ships.

Which vehicle has only one wheel?

In many towns and cities around the world, roads have special bicycle lanes so that cyclists are safe from the other traffic.

Can you spot these things?

juggling balls · cake · silver helmet · sheep · television

The world's busiest airport is in Atlanta, USA. An aircraft takes off or lands there every 37 seconds.

Can you spot these things?

pink suitcase

pilot

crate

toy bunny

Mexican hat

More to spot

Go back and find these scenes in the book!

Did you find me?

Did you Know?

A plane's wings may look solid, but they are designed to bend. The tips bend upwards when the plane takes off.

Sailors call the right side of a ship or boat 'starboard' and the left side 'port'.

On average, a person will spend around two weeks of their life waiting at traffic lights.

REMOVALS

The very first trains were pulled by horses and were used to move coal from mines.

New York, USA, is the city with the most underground train stations in the world — it has 468 in total.

More fun on the move!

Sailing boat

Cut a triangle from stiff paper and make three holes down one side. Weave a drinking straw through the holes to make a sail. Stick modelling clay to the bottom of the straw then fix your sail onto the bottom of a plastic container. Now float your sailing boat on water!

Alphabet game

When you are on the move, look out for the letters of the alphabet on signs or car number plates. Can you find all the letters of the alphabet in order, from A to Z, before your journey ends?

Hide and seek

Choose a cuddly toy that you can hide around your home for a friend or family member to spot, just like the mouse in this book! You could hide other objects too and make a list of things to find.

Cardboard bus

Paint a cardboard box or cover it with coloured paper. Paint or draw wheels and windows onto the sides. Cut out pictures of people's heads and shoulders from magazines and stick them onto the windows.

Design: Duck Egg Blue and Mike Henson
Editors: Tasha Percy and Sophie Hallam
Editorial Director: Victoria Garrard
Art Director: Laura Roberts-Jensen

Copyright © QED Publishing 2015

First published in the UK in 2015 by
QED Publishing
Part of The Quarto Group
The Old Brewery,
6 Blundell Street,
London, N7 9BH

www.qed-publishing.co.uk

A catalogue record for this book is available from the British Library.

ISBN 978 1 78493 091 2

Printed in China